SPORTS GREAT BARRY SANDERS

Revised Edition

—Sports Great Books—

BASEBALL

Sports Great Jim Abbott
0-89490-395-0/ Savage

Sports Great Bobby Bonilla
0-89490-417-5/ Knapp

Sports Great Orel Hershiser
0-89490-389-6/ Knapp

Sports Great Bo Jackson
0-89490-281-4/ Knapp

Sports Great Greg Maddux
0-89490-873-1/ Thornley

Sports Great Kirby Puckett
0-89490-392-6/ Aaseng

Sports Great Cal Ripken, Jr.
0-89490-387-X/ Macnow

Sports Great Nolan Ryan
0-89490-394-2/ Lace

Sports Great Darryl Strawberry
0-89490-291-1/ Torres & Sullivan

BASKETBALL

Sports Great Charles Barkley
Revised Edition
0-7660-1004-X/ Macnow

Sports Great Larry Bird
0-89490-368-3/ Kavanagh

Sports Great Muggsy Bogues
0-89490-876-6/ Rekela

Sports Great Patrick Ewing
0-89490-369-1/ Kavanagh

Sports Great Anfernee Hardaway
0-89490-758-1/ Rekela

Sports Great Juwan Howard
0-7660-1065-1/ Savage

Sports Great Magic Johnson
Revised and Expanded
0-89490-348-9/ Haskins

Sports Great Michael Jordan
Revised Edition
0-89490-978-9/ Aaseng

Sports Great Jason Kidd
0-7660-1001-5/ Torres

Sports Great Karl Malone
0-89490-599-6/ Savage

Sports Great Reggie Miller
0-89490-874-X/ Thornley

Sports Great Alonzo Mourning
0-89490-875-8/ Fortunato

Sports Great Hakeem Olajuwon
0-89490-372-1/ Knapp

Sports Great Shaquille O'Neal
Revised Edition
0-7660-1003-1/ Sullivan

Sports Great Scottie Pippen
0-89490-755-7/ Bjarkman

Sports Great Mitch Richmond
0-7660-1070-8/ Grody

Sports Great David Robinson
Revised Edition
0-7660-1077-5/ Aaseng

Sports Great Dennis Rodman
0-89490-759-X/ Thornley

Sports Great John Stockton
0-89490-598-8/ Aaseng

Sports Great Isiah Thomas
0-89490-374-8/ Knapp

Sports Great Chris Webber
0-7660-1069-4/ Macnow

Sports Great Dominique Wilkins
0-89490-754-9/ Bjarkman

FOOTBALL

Sports Great Troy Aikman
0-89490-593-7/ Macnow

Sports Great Jerome Bettis
0-89490-872-3/ Majewski

Sports Great John Elway
0-89490-282-2/ Fox

Sports Great Brett Favre
0-7660-1000-7/ Savage

Sports Great Jim Kelly
0-89490-670-4/ Harrington

Sports Great Joe Montana
0-89490-371-3/ Kavanagh

Sports Great Jerry Rice
0-89490-419-1/ Dickey

Sports Great Barry Sanders
Revised Edition
0-7660-1067-8/ Knapp

Sports Great Deion Sanders
0-7660-1068-6/ Macnow

Sports Great Emmitt Smith
0-7660-1002-3/ Grabowski

Sports Great Herschel Walker
0-89490-207-5/ Benagh

OTHER

Sports Great Michael Chang
0-7660-1223-9/ Ditchfield

Sports Great Oscar De La Hoya
0-7660-1066-X/ Torres

Sports Great Steffi Graf
0-89490-597-X/ Knapp

Sports Great Wayne Gretzky
0-89490-757-3/ Rappoport

Sports Great Mario Lemieux
0-89490-596-1/ Knapp

Sports Great Eric Lindros
0-89490-871-5/ Rappoport

Sports Great Pete Sampras
0-89490-756-5/ Sherrow

SPORTS GREAT
BARRY SANDERS

Revised Edition

Ron Knapp

—Sports Great Books—

SOUTH HUNTINGTON
PUBLIC LIBRARY
2 MELVILLE ROAD
HUNTINGTON STATION, N.Y. 11746

Enslow Publishers, Inc.

40 Industrial Road	PO Box 38
Box 398	Aldershot
Berkeley Heights, NJ 07922	Hants GU12 6BP
USA	UK

http://www.enslow.com

JB
Sanders
Knapp

Copyright © 1999 by Ron Knapp

All rights reserved.

No part of this book may be reproduced by any means
without the written permission of the publisher.

Library of Congress Cataloging-in-Publication Data

Knapp, Ron.
    Sports great Barry Sanders / Ron Knapp. — Rev. ed.
       p. cm. — (Sports great books)
    Includes index.
    Summary: A biography emphasizing the career of the star running back of the
Detroit Lions football team.
    ISBN 0-7660-1067-8
    1. Sanders, Barry, 1968– —Juvenile literature. 2. Football players—United
States—Biography—Juvenile literature. 3. Detroit Lions (Football team)—History—
Juvenile literature. 4. Football players. [1. Sanders, Barry, 1968– .
2. Afro-Americans—Biography.] I. Title. II. Series.
GV939.S18K6 1999
796.332'092—dc21
[b]   98-14394
                                             CIP
                                             AC

Printed in the United States of America

10 9 8 7 6 5 4 3

To Our Readers: We have done our best to make sure all Internet addresses in this book were
active and appropriate when we went to press. However, the author and the publisher have no
control over and assume no liability for the material available on those Internet sites or on
other Web sites they may link to. Any comments or suggestions can be sent by e-mail to
comments@enslow.com or to the address on the back cover.

Illustration Credits: Amy E. Powers, pp. 18, 25, 35, 41, 45; © Mitchell Layton,
pp. 9, 11, 14, 32, 38, 48, 50, 54, 57, 59; North High School, Wichita, Kansas, pp.
20, 22; Oklahoma State University, pp. 27, 30.

Cover Illustration: © Mitchell Layton

30652001039439

Contents

Chapter 1

Football fans are accustomed to flamboyant running backs. It's not enough for these stars to dodge the defense and race into the end zone. They have to celebrate touchdowns by spiking the ball and dancing. Some of them even jump into the stands.

Not Barry Sanders. When the Detroit Lions' superstar back crosses the goal line, he flips the ball to an official, trots off the field, and sits down.

Some sports stars brag about their accomplishments. They want to remind the fans how good they are. Not Barry Sanders. "I've tried, really, in every play, every game just to compete," is how he explains his success. "And for whatever reason, things have allowed me to be successful. I've had a lot of help from teammates." After his rookie season, Sanders thanked the members of his offensive line for their blocking by giving each of them a ten-thousand-dollar Rolex watch.

Some stars are more concerned with their own individual achievements, not the good of the team. Not Barry Sanders. When he won the 1996 National Football League (NFL) rushing title, he said, "I am proud to say I won the rushing title, but in the big picture I'd rather my teammates and I were playing next week [in the playoffs]."

Many football stars are able to compete in the championship games and win Super Bowl titles with their teams. Not Barry Sanders in 1996. It was his eighth season with the Lions, a team that was expected to be a Super Bowl contender. A year earlier, they had posted the best offensive statistics in the NFL, but 1996 would be a completely different story.

While the Lions were falling apart and their fans were paying attention to other, contending, teams, Sanders was quietly having another incredible season. Against Tampa Bay, linemen Mike Compton and Ray Roberts opened a hole, and Sanders took off for 54 yards and a touchdown. "Once Barry gets in the secondary, he's gone," said Lions coach Wayne Fontes.

When they played Green Bay, the Lions had a third-and-fifteen situation from the Packers 18-yard line. Sanders took the handoff, then slammed head-on into Packers safety Eugene Robinson. The play should have been dead there, but Barry bounced off the bigger man and took off before he could be tackled. Seeing an opening, he cut across the field. Seven Packers had a shot at him as he raced into the end zone, but none of them could bring him down.

In 1996, the only thing that ever really stopped Sanders was Detroit's own strategy. Early in the season, the Lions got behind early in most games, then gave up on their running game to concentrate on passes for quick touchdowns. Against Oakland, Sanders carried the ball only 9 times. But the passing strategy did not work. Quarterback Scott Mitchell had trouble connecting with his receivers, and once they got behind, the Lions rarely came back.

Before the November 17, 1996, game with Seattle, Fontes decided to change tactics. "We talked about Barry all week," he said. "I said, 'Even if we get behind, we've got to keep getting

Barry Sanders finds some open space and runs for the end zone.

the ball to Barry.' The more he runs it, the better he gets. We want to get him the ball between 15 and 20 times."

Against Seattle, Sanders got the ball 16 times and gained 134 yards. The Lions won, 17–16. Backup quarterback Don Majkowski liked the new strategy. "Our whole offense is built around No. 20. He is just an unbelievable talent. . . . Barry Sanders is by far the best running back in football."

The next week even 107 Sanders yards in 21 carries were not enough to save Detroit from being trounced, 31–14, by Chicago. That yardage raised his 1996 total to over 1,000, making him the first running back in NFL history to gain over 1,000 yards in eight consecutive seasons. It also put him ahead of O. J. Simpson in career rushing totals, placing Sanders eighth on the all-time standings. Simpson had 11,236 yards in eleven years. Sanders had passed him in his eighth season.

Why was he so good? The question made Sanders uncomfortable. "I feel fortunate," he said. "I've been consistent and stayed healthy." It was left to Fontes to do the bragging: "Barry's the best back to ever touch the football."

Sanders, as usual, was more interested in talking about the team. Instead of being excited about his own totals, he said he was frustrated and disappointed at his team's 5–7 record. "But we have to keep fighting. We have to show pride in ourselves. We have four really tough games left. We can't give up."

Unfortunately, that seemed to be what some of his teammates were doing. Morale and team spirit were sinking. Players got sloppy at practice and in the games. Why bother to try when the team was having a lousy year? Several players publicly blamed Fontes for the losses. The Lions seemed to be a sinking ship.

Detroit's offensive line was not always strong, so sometimes Sanders faced a wall of would-be tacklers as soon as he got the ball. On many plays he did not have much help; he had

Although Sanders is surrounded by Jets defenders, he is still able to break free for a big gain.

to get the yards himself. "Sanders could take the worst play in the world and he could be out the other side [of the field] in a second," said Tony Wise, offensive line coach of the Chicago Bears.

Sports broadcaster John Madden agreed: "The first guy doesn't get [him]. Neither does the second. It's usually the fourth or fifth guy."

Despite the team's problems, Sanders kept on fighting. As the Lions fell, 28–24, to Kansas City, he picked up 77 yards in 20 tries. On the first play from scrimmage against the Minnesota Vikings on December 8, he broke through for 12 yards. On the next play, he took the ball another 10. At that point, he passed John Riggins, who had gained 11,352 yards in his fifteen-year career. Now Sanders was No. 7 on the NFL career rushing list. He gained 134 yards that day against the Vikings, but Detroit lost, 24–22.

Going into the final game of the regular season, a Monday night match against the mighty San Francisco 49ers, Detroit had lost eight of its last nine games. Even though he was playing on such a mediocre team, Sanders had an amazing 1,378 rushing yards for the season. That put him second in the National Football Conference (NFC) to Ricky Watters' 1,411. Leading the league was Denver's Terrell Davis, the AFC leader, at 1,538.

Most Detroit fans had no hope that their team could beat the 49ers. Like most of the Lions, they were just glad to see the disastrous season finally coming to an end. Virtually the only bright spot had been Sanders. With just one more good day, he could set another NFL record. If he gained 122 yards, he would become the first player ever to rush for 1,500 yards in three consecutive seasons. In fact, a great day might put him within reach of Davis and the 1996 rushing title.

Most observers gave him little chance against San Francisco. The 49ers had one of the league's toughest defenses against the run. In the previous twenty-one games, only one back had gained 100 or more yards against them. That was Pittsburgh's Erric Pegram, who got just 103 the week before. Besides, the Lions would probably fall behind early. What if Fontes went back to his old strategy of concentrating on passing to get back into the game?

And what about the rest of the team? Many of the other players were publicly complaining about their poor season and putting the blame on Fontes. Mitchell even ridiculed his coach by dressing up like him at a party. Before the 49er game, reporters asked if he had anything left to play for. "No," the quarterback replied.

Barry Sanders had plenty to play for. He showed up in San

Francisco ready to fight. Early in the game, he grabbed the ball at midfield and headed right. Blocking his way was 49ers safety Tim McDonald. A couple of fakes, and Sanders was by him. Quickly, he cut back across the field. Dedrick Dodge grabbed him, but Sanders spun, and he was free.

Now he was in the secondary, and there were only two defenders between him and a touchdown. It was no contest. As Fontes pointed out, once Sanders is past the line, it's all over. It was a 54-yard run against the playoff-bound 49ers.

"That guy was totally amazing," was all McDonald could say.

Sanders was not finished. As Detroit sank further and further behind, he kept piling up the yardage. When time ran out, San Francisco had won, 24–14, but he had picked up 175 yards in 28 carries.

With that effort, Sanders became the first man in NFL history to get at least 1,500 yards for each of three straight years. His total of 1,553 yards also put him past Watters and Davis for the season rushing title.

Of course, when the game ended, Sanders did not celebrate his own achievements. He walked over to Fontes and gave him a hug. It was an emotional moment for both men. Fontes knew he was about to be fired, and Sanders knew he was about to lose the only NFL coach he had ever had.

Afterward, Sanders said he was surprised by his own great performance. "I had no reason to believe we could run for that many yards against the 'Niners." Even though his goal had been a playoff spot, he said, "It's fun to win a rushing title. I want to get as many yards in every game as possible." The San Francisco game was especially important because it was Fontes' last.

The 49ers were impressed. "I've never seen him run with more intensity, more determination," said George Seifert, San

Sanders is very proud of the honors he has received, but what he wants more than anything else is for his team to be successful in the playoffs.

Francisco's coach. "We have to pay special tribute to him for a tremendous performance."

Eugene Robinson, safety on the Green Bay Packers, the team that would eventually take the 1996 Super Bowl, told reporters, "Barry Sanders ain't no joke. . . . He's the best back in the universe. He's the Michael Jordan of football. There ain't no doubt. But Barry's just one dude. He can't do it all himself. Great as he is, he's just one guy."

The 1996 playoffs went on without Barry Sanders. Professional football's most exciting runner could only hope his team would do better next season.

Chapter 2

Barry Sanders was born on July 16, 1968, in Wichita, Kansas. He was the seventh child of William and Shirley Sanders. After Barry, there were four more children. He had two brothers and eight sisters.

Mr. and Mrs. Sanders expected their children to behave and stay out of trouble. William Sanders made sure everybody understood the family rules. "My dad always shot straight," Barry said, "[he] didn't beat around the bush." Mr. Sanders worked hard as a carpenter and a roofer, and he expected his children to work hard at school. "We want nice jobs, nice homes, nice cars, but there's no way to get it unless you're educated," he told them.

Mrs. Sanders thought education was important, too. After her children were all in school, she earned a nursing degree from Wichita State University. Also, when Barry and his sisters and brothers were growing up, their mother made sure they attended services at Paradise Baptist Church.

Barry was never a big child. His classmates were almost always taller and heavier than he was. "From fourth grade on," he said, "I was always smaller than most kids." Even though he was little, Barry did not want anybody to think he was not tough. Sometimes he got into fights because he did not let anybody push him around. "I'm not perfect," he said. "When I was younger, people thought I was a bully."

Barry got into his share of trouble. He and his older brother Byron stole candy and threw rocks at cars. Once Barry started a fire on the floor of the bathroom at home.

Like any other big city, Wichita had problems with young people getting into serious trouble. Some teenagers joined violent gangs or began taking drugs, but not Barry. "It's a fine line between going right and wrong. Sometimes I wonder why I've been so fortunate. My oldest brother, Boyd, influenced me a lot." Barry also gives a lot of credit to his parents. "Seeing my mom and dad raise eleven kids, against the odds they faced, gave me confidence in what I could do."

When Barry was still in elementary school, he learned to play football. He and his friends would get together for games after school. Sometimes there were as many as twenty players on each team. Most of them were bigger than Barry. With forty people playing, not many people got a chance to run with the ball. Barry had to prove to his teammates that, even though he was small, he was good enough to be a running back. Once he got his chance to run with the ball, he decided he did not like to be tackled—especially not by kids who were a lot bigger than he was. He tried hard to run around and away from the other team. He began to develop the style that would make him the best college football player in the nation in 1988, and one of the most exciting runners in the history of the NFL.

Barry joined the junior varsity team at North High School when he was in tenth grade. He was fast, and he had good moves; but the coaches didn't think he would be a good running back. Since he was only five feet tall and weighed 120

Throughout his life, other people thought that Sanders would not be a great running back because of his lack of size. He has always proven them wrong.

pounds, they figured he was too small. It would be too easy for the big players on the other teams to tackle him. Barry became a defensive back, but most of the time he had to sit on the bench while the coaches let the bigger boys play.

The next year Barry was on the varsity team with his older brother Byron, who was a starting tailback. The coaches thought that might be a good position for Barry, too, but he refused. He did not want to try to take a spot away from his brother. The coaches let him be a receiver on offense and a cornerback on defense.

Byron was a star on the high school team. He was also Barry's best friend. He encouraged his brother to stay on the team and try to become a better player. It was not easy. Many of the coaches figured that Barry would never be big enough to be a decent player. Byron convinced him not to give up. Byron was such a good player that he was recruited by Northwestern University as a running back. Meanwhile, back in Wichita, it didn't look as if Barry was ever going to get a chance to prove that he could be a fine running back, too. When he started his senior year at North High, Barry was still catching passes and playing cornerback.

Then, after the North Redskins had lost two of their first three games, Coach Dale Burkholder decided to make Sanders the starting tailback. Early in the game Barry took the ball around the left end and went 49 yards for a touchdown. By the time the game was over, he had rushed for 274 yards and 4 touchdowns as North beat the South High Titans, 29–19. The tailback job was his for the rest of the season.

Burkholder loved the way Barry moved on the field: "Call it the 'jukes,' call it the 'shake and bake,' but Barry has the ability to dodge tacklers, and he reads his blocks intelligently." All of a sudden, Barry was the most exciting running back in Wichita. Twice he was named the league's Player of the Week.

Barry did not act like some of the other stars. "Barry was a silent leader," said his teammate Mike Crosby. "After he'd score a touchdown, he wouldn't celebrate. He'd just give the ball to the ref and walk off the field."

Midway through the season, North celebrated homecoming week. The students held pep assemblies and bonfires and wore special clothes on days like Weird Wednesday, Pajama Day, and Cowboy and Indian Day. The highlight of the week came at the Saturday night dance when Barry Sanders, the quiet senior tailback, was named Pigskin Pete, the homecoming king. Barry dressed up for the dance in a green sport coat and a red-and-white crown.

Late in the season, the Redskins met the East Aces, a team they had not beaten in five years. Sanders and Billy Williams each got a pair of third-quarter touchdowns, and it was all over for the Aces. North won, 35–14.

The Redskins' 5–4 season meant they qualified for the Kansas regional playoffs. Burkholder was very proud of his

Barry Sanders was selected as homecoming king during his senior year at North High School in Wichita, Kansas.

team. "We have people playing positions that one would think that they were too small to play," he said. Burkholder's five-foot, eight-inch tailback gave a lot of the credit for his success to his blockers. "I'm thankful that I had a line like them. They worked hard for me, and I tried to make their work pay off."

North met Manhattan in the first game of the playoffs. Trailing 7–0 early in the game, the Redskins drove to the Manhattan 5-yard line. Barry took it in from there, and the game was tied. With Barry running and wingback Todd Breth making a series of diving catches, the Redskins dominated the rest of the game. Breth finished with seven receptions for 100 yards, and Sanders had 150 yards receiving and ran for 2 touchdowns. Late in the game, North led, 14–7.

After adding a field goal, Manhattan had the ball at its own 43-yard line, with fifteen seconds left. The Redskins' fans were ready to count down the seconds when the Manhattan quarterback fired a desperation pass toward the end zone. The pass was caught. Manhattan won, 16–14, and the season was over for North.

It was a disappointing finish for Sanders, but it had been an incredible year. Even though he had only started at tailback in six games, he had rushed for 1,417 yards, an average of 10.2 yards per carry. He was named to the All-City and All-State teams. "Good backs have a combination of speed, strength, and the ability to make people miss," said Burkholder. "Barry has all these. He's the best natural ball carrier I've been around in high school."

Assistant Coach Kyle Sanders (no relation to Barry) was glad to have had Sanders on the team. "It was terribly exciting," he said. "A player like Barry doesn't come around often. He is talented, unselfish, and I hate to see him go."

Barry himself kept trying to give credit to his teammates. "I had real good blocking this season," he said. "They gave me a crack, and I ran through it." Offensive lineman Shawn Sater was glad Sanders finally made it to the backfield. "It was a pleasure to block for a great back like Barry," he said. "He made our work easier. If you put a hole there, he'd hit it."

As soon as the football season was over, Barry and many of the other players headed for the gym to begin basketball practice. Barry was one of the shortest men on the team, but he still got a lot of playing time. His strong legs helped him jump higher than many of the taller players. But even Barry's jumping ability couldn't bring the Redskins a winning record. North lost three games in overtime and four others by two points or less.

Barry was disappointed. "We had talented players," he said, "but we never got everyone playing their best at the same time."

When the basketball season ended, Barry began to concentrate on what he would do after graduation from high school.

In Barry's senior year in high school he averaged 10.2 yards per carry.

He hoped he could follow in his brother Byron's footsteps and get a football scholarship to a major university. His high school coach encouraged him. "Barry has that 'hang in there' attitude it takes to make it in [a] major college."

It would be nice, Barry thought, to be able to choose from many different colleges, but he was disappointed. Very few college coaches were interested in him.

The problem with Barry was not his talent or his desire to work hard. The problem was still his size. When he graduated from Wichita North High School in 1986, he was still only five-feet eight-inches tall, and he weighed 180 pounds. Many of the defensive players at the major colleges were much taller and heavier. The college coaches figured Barry was just too small to play for them. As one of them said, "We didn't need another midget."

Only two schools offered him scholarships—Wichita State in his hometown and Oklahoma State University (OSU) in Stillwater, Oklahoma. Barry knew he was good enough to play for the major college teams. "It's amazing to me how much attention coaches and scouts pay to size," he said. "The fact that most of the big schools ignored me gave me incentive to show them that it's not all about size."

Barry accepted the scholarship from Oklahoma State. When he left Wichita, he was ready to prove that he belonged in college football.

Chapter 3

When Barry Sanders arrived at Oklahoma State University in Stillwater in the late summer of 1986, the Cowboys already had a star running back in Thurman Thomas. During his freshman year, Sanders carried the ball in only six games. His best performance was against Illinois State, when he gained 132 yards in 25 carries. By the end of the season, he had only 325 yards in 74 attempts.

It was not until his sophomore year at Oklahoma State that Sanders finally got a chance to sparkle. In the first game against Tulsa, he took the opening kickoff 100 yards, for a touchdown.

During the 1987 season, Sanders was the best kickoff returner in the country. He had 470 yards in 15 returns, an average of 31.3 yards per carry. He also had a few more chances to show what he could do in the Cowboy backfield. Late in the season, he ran 105 yards against Kansas State, 116 against Kansas, and 124 against Iowa State. That gave him 654 yards for the season in 111 carries, an average of 5.9 yards per carry.

Once Sanders finds some room to run, his speed allows him to pull away from his defenders. In college, Sanders was so quick that the coach even used him to return kickoffs.

Sanders became OSU's top running back in 1988 after Thomas left for the Buffalo Bills, of the National Football League. Once again, Sanders started off the season with a bang. Against Miami, he took the opening kickoff from one end zone to the other, for a 100-yard touchdown return. That made him the first college player ever to open two seasons in a row with kickoff return touchdowns. Then, in the backfield, he ran the ball 18 times, for 182 yards.

Two weeks later, against Tulsa, he ran for 310 yards and 5 touchdowns. When the Cowboys met the Colorado Buffaloes in the fourth game of the season, both teams were undefeated. Colorado scored first, but then OSU drove to the one-yard line. Sanders popped through the line for a touchdown. A few minutes later, he leaped high over the Buffalo line from a yard out and landed in the end zone. Before the half ended, he took another handoff at the 7-yard line and made his way through a crowd of Buffaloes, over the goal line.

The next time he got the ball, Sanders swept quickly around the end. All of a sudden, he was all by himself, so he took off for the end zone, sixty-five yards away. "That play broke their backs," said OSU coach Pat Jones. When the game ended, Sanders had 4 touchdowns and 174 yards rushing.

Sanders' "worst" game of the season came two weeks later against Missouri when he gained 154 yards in 25 carries. The next week he ran for 320 yards and scored 3 touchdowns against Kansas State.

After he rushed for 215 yards and a pair of touchdowns against Oklahoma, there was a lot of talk about Sanders' being a serious contender for the Heisman Trophy, the annual award given each year to the finest college football player in the nation.

As far as Sanders was concerned, the important thing about sports was doing your best to win, not collecting individual honors. He said he did not care about the Heisman. The only important thing was for the team to win. When reporters praised his running, he tried to share the glory with his teammates. "The offensive line played so well, they made everything easy."

Sanders did not like to brag or show off. He was still a shy person who did not enjoy making speeches or talking to reporters. After he made a touchdown, he did not jump around or spike the ball. He just handed it to a referee and trotted off the field. It was not his style to get too excited. After all, he figured football was just a game. "People take sports way too seriously," he said. "To some of them, sports is a god, which is wrong."

Against Kansas, he put on one of the most explosive performances in the history of college football. Before halftime, he scored on runs of 4, 8, 20, and 21 yards. In 25 carries he rushed for 217 yards—and he still had a half to go. Sanders spent much of the second half on the bench because the Cowboys

Barry Sanders played his college football for the Oklahoma State University Cowboys.

were so far ahead. He did score another touchdown, and finished the day with 312 yards on 37 carries. OSU won, 63–24.

Sanders' performance against Kansas meant that in the first nine games he had scored 31 touchdowns, two more than any other college player. His season rushing total stood at 2,003 yards, making him only the third running back in the history of college football to run for more than 2,000 yards. OSU coach Jones reminded reporters that Sanders still had two games left to play in the regular season.

The following week Sanders made 4 touchdowns and ran 293 more yards against Iowa State. That gave him 2,296 yards rushing for the season, second only to Marcus Allen's 2,342 at the University of Southern California in 1986. If he could get just forty-seven yards against the Texas Tech Red Raiders, he would be the leading rusher in the history of college football. That game would be played in Tokyo, Japan, on December 3, just a few hours after the winner of the Heisman Trophy was announced in New York City.

Sanders and quarterbacks Rodney Peete of USC and Troy Aikman of UCLA were the leading candidates for the Heisman. Peete and Aikman would be at the award ceremony in New York City, but Sanders would be in a Tokyo television studio so American viewers could watch his reaction when the award was announced. A few of his teammates came along to keep him company.

Hardly anybody was surprised when the announcement came that Sanders was the winner. His teammates cheered, but once again Sanders did not want to show off. He barely smiled as he said, "I'd like to thank God for putting me in this position. . . . I would also like to thank my offensive line."

A few hours later, Sanders took a pitch out from quarterback Mike Gundy, broke three tackles, and ran 56 yards for a touchdown. A few minutes later he turned a short pass reception into a 66-yard gain. By the end of the game, he had given the Japanese fans a great exhibition of American football. He had run for 257 yards and 4 touchdowns, as the Cowboys beat Texas Tech, 45–42.

In the Holiday Bowl four weeks later, against Wyoming, Oklahoma State had a slim 24–14 lead midway through the third quarter. Sanders broke the game open when he took the ball on his own 33-yard line. Three Wyoming players grabbed him, but he shook them off as he ran 67 yards for a touchdown. Later, on an option, he surprised everybody by completing a 17-yard pass to Gundy. Sanders scored again on a one-yard run, and the OSU lead was a safe 38–14. By the end of the game, Sanders had 222 yards and 5 touchdowns, and the Cowboys had a 62–14 victory.

Nobody had ever had a season like the one Sanders had in 1988. In 344 carries, he had taken the ball a record 2,628 yards. His total yardage, 39 touchdowns, and 234 total points were also records.

With the season finally over, Sanders had time to think about his future. He had finished three years at Oklahoma State, which meant that he could still play for one more season. Now that he had won the Heisman Trophy, he had another option. He was talented enough to play professionally in the NFL.

At first, Sanders thought he would remain at Oklahoma State for his senior year. "Mentally, I don't feel I'm ready for a job [in the NFL]," he said. "Physically, I may want to gain five more pounds." But what about all the money he could make in the NFL? If Sanders signed a professional contract, he would become an instant millionaire. Until now, he had never really been interested in money. He did not wear fancy jewelry as some other athletes did, and he drove a beat-up old car, not a fancy sports model.

Charging through the defensive line, Barry Sanders surges toward another first down. Sanders set many NCAA records during his career at Oklahoma State University.

Then two things happened. Soon after the Holiday Bowl, the National Collegiate Athletic Association (NCAA) announced that Oklahoma State would be punished for breaking recruiting rules. During the 1989 season, the Cowboys team could not appear on television and would not be allowed to participate in postseason bowl games. If Sanders stayed at OSU, he would not be seen by many fans or pro coaches. They might forget about him.

At about the same time, his dad, William Sanders, began trying to convince his son that the family could use the cash. "We can have money in our family for generations to come—for your kids and your kids' kids." Mr. Sanders tried to convince Barry to leave college. "You'd be crazy to go back and play at Oklahoma State. Why play eleven games for free when you can play sixteen games for millions of dollars? Get out of school so we can all get on with our lives."

Barry's mother, Shirley Sanders, did not want her son to quit college. She wanted him to graduate before he signed a professional contract. If he left school now, it would be very hard for him to go back.

That kind of talk exasperated Mr. Sanders. He was worried that Barry might be injured playing another season at OSU. If that happened, he wouldn't be able to make any money from the NFL.

Sanders listened to the advice and then made his decision. In April he told reporters that it had been hard to do any schoolwork since he had won the Heisman Trophy. He was still trying to finish semester final tests from December. With all the attention from the press, it was almost impossible to keep up with his classes. He had decided it was time to leave OSU for the NFL.

William Sanders was a relieved, happy man. He hoped that his son's pro contract would be signed quickly and that the big checks would soon be on their way. But first Barry Sanders had to be chosen in the NFL draft. Some of the teams were still worried about his size. Was he really big enough to make it in the NFL?

The Detroit Lions decided to check Sanders out. Coach Wayne Fontes had never seen him play. "Of course, in all the film we saw, we never saw anybody catch him," he said. "That should have told us something." Fontes went to Oklahoma to see if Sanders was as good as he looked on film. On the track, Sanders demonstrated his speed, running 40 yards in just 4.39 seconds. Then he showed his leg strength by jumping straight up 41.5 inches. When Fontes saw that jump, he was sure he wanted Sanders on his team.

When Sanders was coming out of college, Lions coach Wayne Fontes liked what he saw. Detroit signed Sanders after drafting him with the third pick of the 1989 NFL draft.

Sanders' agents and the Lions negotiated for weeks on his contract. Training camp opened, but he had not yet signed a contract so he did not report. It was not until three days before the first game that an agreement was reached. Sanders' first NFL contract was good for $6.1 million over five years.

As soon as he got his first check, he sent $210,000 to Paradise Baptist Church, his church back in Wichita. "I was kind of awestruck when I found out," said Reverend Michael Frost, the church's assistant pastor. "Barry's been brought up to give. I expected him to do something. But nothing of this magnitude."

Sanders concentrated on getting ready for his rookie season in the NFL. "I'm not one to make promises," he said. "But I'm ready to give 100 percent to the Detroit Lions. It's time to work. This is big business."

Chapter 4

The Silverdome in Pontiac, Michigan, could hold eighty thousand football fans, but only 36,735 of the seats were filled for Barry Sanders' first NFL game. Detroit fans did not expect much from the Lions. The team had never played in a Super Bowl. In fact, the Lions had not even had a winning season since 1982.

The fans in the half-empty Silverdome went wild when Sanders trotted onto the field. It was early in the game, but the Lions already trailed the Phoenix Cardinals, 6–3. On his first play as a pro, Sanders watched the Lions get a big break when Michael Zordich of the Cardinals was called for pass interference on Jason Phillips. That took the ball to the Cardinals 29-yard line.

On the next play, Sanders broke loose for 18 yards. The Lions fans gave him another tremendous ovation. Detroit had the ball on the 11-yard line. Quarterback Bob Gagliano again handed the ball off to Sanders, who carried it three yards. Then he carried it to the 3-yard line. It was third down and two yards to go.

Barry Sanders quickly became one of the most exciting runners in the
National Football League.

Nobody was surprised when Sanders got the ball for the fourth play in a row. He broke a tackle by Zordich and slipped into the corner of the end zone. The Lions led, and their fans loved it. Maybe Sanders was the man who could turn the Lions into winners.

Lions coach Wayne Fontes did not think Sanders was ready to play full time yet, so the rookie only carried the ball five more times. His longest gain was a 25-yarder that set up a tying field goal by Eddie Murray late in the game. But the Lions still lost, 16–13, when Al Del Greco kicked a field goal for the Cardinals with just thirteen seconds left.

Sanders was disappointed about the outcome of the game, but happy that he was finally playing. "It just felt good to be out and running and playing football," he said.

Fontes was pleased with his new player. "He's everything we thought he was. Everyone knew he was going to carry the ball, and he still did what he did. Hopefully, he'll make me a great coach."

When the season started, Sanders barely knew his teammates. After all, he had not practiced with the team until he had signed his contract three days before the first game. Some of his teammates were not sure they would like him. He had gotten a lot of attention because he was the Heisman Trophy winner who had become an instant millionaire by signing a pro contract. Some of the other Lions did not like having the spotlight focused on a rookie. They had also heard that he was a quiet, religious man who had given thousands of dollars to his church. Would he spend his time in the locker room reading the Bible to his teammates and trying to talk them into going to church?

There was not much time to worry about what kind of a man Sanders was, because the team still had fifteen games left to play in the season. In the next game, Sanders ran the ball 12 times for 57 yards. The Lions lost again, 24–14, to the New York Giants.

Next, Sanders had his best game so far, gaining 126 yards in 18 tries against the Chicago Bears, but he had to sit out the end of the game after bruising his hip in the third quarter. The Lions lost to the Bears, 47–27. Sanders said he was improving. "I read blocks better this week. I felt I had a pretty productive day, but it could've been better."

By that time, the other Lions were getting used to having Sanders around, and they were beginning to like him. He noticed that Coach Fontes kept a Bible on his desk. Every few days Sanders would suggest a different verse for his coach to read. Fontes would nod and promise to read it, then change the subject. After a few weeks, Sanders pointed to the Bible and said, "Coach, you haven't been reading this." How did he know? Sanders pointed at the bookmark and said, "Because this hasn't moved since August."

His religion was important to him, but in a quiet sort of way. Sanders did not make speeches about the Bible or argue with his teammates about going to church. "He doesn't wear his beliefs on his sleeve," Fontes said. "Barry's not the type of guy who scores a TD and kneels down in front of everyone in the world. He's not for show, he's for real."

Sanders also won friends on the Lions with his sense of humor. During one of his first practices with the team, he walked off the field and told Fontes, "I don't know if I can go back in there."

The coach was worried. "What's wrong?" he asked. "Are you hurt?"

"No. But the guys are using some awfully foul language out there. I don't know if I can stand it." Fontes didn't know what to say. Football players have a reputation for using rough language. What could he do with a superstar who refused to

Sanders is a quiet and hardworking man who does not like to brag.

listen to people who swore? Finally Sanders began laughing and ran back to the huddle. It was just a joke. Fontes breathed a sigh of relief and laughed, too.

The Lions got a kick out of Sanders' joke, but they enjoyed his playing even more. "He's awesome when he runs," said tackle Lomas Brown. "You can't explain how it is to block for him. You don't have to hold your block long. He just makes it fun to play."

The other players also discovered that despite all the attention Sanders got from reporters and fans, he never bragged or tried to act as if he was better or more important than his teammates. "I've always been one of the guys as long as I've played football," he said. "I guess nobody told me to be any other way."

The Lions were getting along well among themselves, but they still were not doing very well on the football field. They were winless in their first five games, and they were in trouble in the next one. With twenty-three seconds left and Sanders back on the bench with his injured hip, Detroit trailed Tampa Bay, 16–9. Then, rookie quarterback Rodney Peete scrambled into the end zone from the 5-yard line to give Detroit the win.

Sanders was back in action two weeks later against Green Bay. He gained 184 yards in 30 carries, but the Lions still lost in overtime, 23–20. Then they lost another close one to Houston, 35–31. Detroit's record was 1–8.

The Lions jumped out to a 24–3 halftime lead against the Packers, but then Green Bay made it 24–20. It looked as if the Lions were going to blow another one. Finally, they got a break when a Green Bay fumble was recovered by linebacker Chris Spielman and returned to the Packer 41–yard line.

Fontes and his assistant coaches had to decide what plays to run. Everybody seemed to have a different idea, but then Fontes settled the question by yelling, "I don't care what you do—just give it to Barry." That's what Peete did, and Sanders took it 11 yards for a first down. After two more short gains by Sanders, Peete flipped him a swing pass that was flying over his head, but Sanders jumped, made a one-handed catch, and took the ball to the 5-yard line. "That catch by Barry was the turning point in the game for us," Fontes said. "Rodney threw the ball a little high, and Barry made a great catch."

On the next play, Sanders went 4 yards over left tackle to the one-yard line. Then, on an option play, Peete lateraled the ball to him, and he slipped untouched over the goal line. That touchdown gave Detroit a 31–20 victory and helped begin to turn the season around.

Cincinnati clobbered Detroit, 42–7. But the next week, Sanders picked up 145 yards, and the Lions upset the Bears, 13–10. "We haven't been able to win much," Sanders said, "but we've been competitive. Hopefully we showed the rest of the country that we're not a bad team. People can say we're three–nine, but we're not a bad team."

After beating New Orleans, 21–14, the Lions surprised Chicago again, 27–17. Sanders gained 120 yards and scored 2 touchdowns. "I feel great about this team," said Fontes. It was the first time in five years that Detroit had won three in a row. Then the Lions bombed Tampa Bay, 33–7. "At this point," said nose tackle Jerry Ball, "we're playing the best ball in the league." Sanders gained 104 yards, giving him 1,308 for the year, the most ever by a Detroit rookie.

In the final game of the season against the Atlanta Falcons, the Lions jumped off to an early lead. Sanders got a second-quarter touchdown on a 25-yard run, then had scoring runs of 17 and 19 yards in the second half. That gave him 14 rushing touchdowns for the season. He had also gained 158 yards, to raise his season-rushing total to 1,470.

With a minute to go, the Lions had the ball and a 31–24

After a hard-fought series of downs, Barry Sanders heads for the sideline.

lead. Sanders already had ran for 158 yards and 3 touchdowns, enough to give him 1,470 yards and 14 touchdowns for the season, both Lions records. He had something else to shoot for. Christian Okoye had just finished the season with a league-leading total of 1,480 yards for the Kansas City Chiefs. That meant Sanders was just eleven yards short of winning the league rushing championship. "You're ten yards from leading the league in rushing," Fontes told his star. "Do you want to go in?"

Sanders did not seem to care about the title. "Coach, let's just win it and go home." Fontes asked him if he would get a cash bonus for leading the league. Sanders did not care. "Coach," he said, "give the ball to Tony [Paige]. Let's win it and go home." So Sanders stayed on the bench, the Lions ran out the clock, and Okoye won the rushing title. That did not bother Sanders. The most important thing was that the Lions had finished the season with five straight victories. After a rough start, they were one of the hottest teams in the league. They were looking forward to 1990.

Chapter 5

After the great finish in 1989, the Lions and their fans were very disappointed when the team lost three of its first four games in 1990. Coach Wayne Fontes had decided to concentrate on Rodney Peete's passing, so Barry Sanders did not get the ball much. In those three losses, he had only gained a total of 186 yards.

Sanders scored 2 touchdowns when Detroit beat Minnesota, 34–27, and he was hot the next week in Kansas City. Early in the game he caught a short screen pass from backup quarterback Bob Gagliano, faked out two Chiefs, and ran 47 yards, for his longest pro touchdown. Minutes later he scored again, this time on a 13-yard run. Detroit led, 14–3. Then it was the Chiefs' turn to get hot. Kansas City made two quick touchdowns to take the lead, 17–14, at the half. By the end of the game, the Lions had been buried, 43–24. "We got our tails whipped," said Fontes. "We were a bad football team, and as a whole, we stunk." Sanders had been the only bright spot for Detroit. He had 90 yards rushing and picked up 135 yards on 5 pass receptions, his best so far in the NFL. Sanders still did not really care about his yardage or his records. "Statistics usually get in the way of team goals," he said, "and satisfied athletes don't get better." And what good was it to get a lot of yards if the team kept losing?

The Lions lost two of the next three games, and most of the time Sanders still was not getting the ball as he had in 1989. That made the owner of the Lions angry. "Barry is a super talent," said William Clay Ford. "There are twenty-seven other teams out there who wish they had him. It's criminal not to use him." Fontes listened to Ford and decided it was time to base the Lions' offense on Sanders. Sanders came through, rushing 23 times for 147 yards as Detroit dropped Denver, 40–27. "Barry Sanders is just unbelievable," said Broncos coach Dan Reeves. "He had a great game, and we just couldn't contain him."

Sanders was happy with that game. "It felt good to be more involved," he said. "We needed to get a win." By that time, Detroit's record was 4–7. Two weeks later he had 176 yards against the Los Angeles Raiders. His performance pushed his season rushing total to 1,081, making him only the tenth back in NFL history to get more than 1,000 yards in each of his first two pro seasons. "The more we give Barry the ball, the better off we are," said Fontes. But the Lions still lost, 38–31.

Early in a game against Green Bay, Sanders fumbled the ball away at the Packers 13-yard line. "I really wanted to get back in there and get the ball and just build my confidence back up," he said, and that is just what he did. Late in the game with the score tied, 17–17, he got the ball on a trap and ran 37 yards back to the Green Bay 13-yard line. After being stopped at the line, then going 6 yards, he raced around the right end for 6 yards and the winning touchdown with 3:37 left. His final rushing total for the game was 133 yards, pushing his league-leading season total to 1,281 yards with one game left. Reporters kept asking him if Fontes had been wrong not to use

Barry Sanders struggles to break free from the clutches of a defender.

him more often earlier in the season. "I think they tried to do what they thought was best to win games," he said. There was no need to whine about not getting the ball. "That would make it seem like I'm taking a personal jab at the staff."

The Lions ended their disappointing season by losing to the Seattle Seahawks, 30–10, and Sanders carried the ball only 9 times, for 23 yards. But that was enough to give him 1,304 for the season, tops in the league. Finishing just behind him with 1,297 was Buffalo's Thurman Thomas, the man he had replaced at Oklahoma State University. Sanders did not make a big deal about winning the rushing title. He would rather have helped the Lions make it into the playoffs, but instead they ended the season with a 6–10 record.

Fontes and the rest of the Lions were criticized for another losing season, but hardly anybody had anything bad to say about Sanders. His teammates did not seem to mind that he got so much credit or that he made so much money. They joked that the only thing they did not like about him was that he was always hungry and never seemed to have any food of his own. After a practice or a game, he bummed food off his teammates. He was a familiar sight at punter Jim Arnold's locker asking for cookies. As he gobbled them down, he would say, "Um, yo, thanks a lot, man."

"The man is a little thief," joked noseguard Jerry Ball. "He comes over to my house almost every night and steals food. One of the highest-paid players in the game, and he eats me out of house and home. He hasn't got an ounce of food in his own icebox."

The 1991 season opened disastrously. Sanders' bruised ribs kept him out of the game, and Detroit was whipped by the Washington Redskins, 45–0. He was back the next week, picking up only 42 yards on 18 carries against Green Bay, but that was enough. Peete said, "The linebackers have to hold up to see if he gets the ball, and that opens up the passing game." Peete gave Sanders the credit, but Peete had the great game, completing 25 passes for 271 yards. Detroit won, 23–14.

In the next game, the Lions were leading Miami, 17–13; but there was still 2:58 left, and Detroit had the ball at its own 5-yard line. The Lions had to keep control of the ball to ensure the victory. Peete passed to Robert Clark for a 15-yard gain and a first down. Three plays later Sanders hit the line and was going nowhere. "He didn't have the first down initially," said Peete, "but he squirted out the other side of that big pileup." Sanders' 3 yards on that play were good enough for a first down. Detroit held the ball and won the game.

Sanders had 179 yards and 2 touchdowns as Detroit beat Indianapolis, 33–24, but he tried to give the credit to his linemen. "We were blowing them off the ball," he said. "The creases were very, very easy to read and to find the last couple of drives." He did not want to talk about his yardage. "We're trying to shoot for some division respect." He wanted the Lions to keep winning.

Detroit won its fourth in a row, clobbering Tampa Bay, 31–3, as Sanders scored 3 touchdowns and rushed for 160 yards. Then, the Lions raised their record to 5–1 by coming from behind to beat Minnesota, 24–20.

In the Lions' next game, Sanders only gained 26 yards as the San Francisco 49ers blasted the Lions, 35–3. Were the Lions going to go back to their old familiar losing ways? No way, said Fontes. "We're not the same old Lions. We're not going to fold our tents. It's just a loss." He was right. The Lions looked tough the next week, beating the Dallas Cowboys, 34–10, and giving the Silverdome crowd something to cheer about. "Today we were ready to play," the coach said.

Then came losses to the Bears and the Buccaneers, and the Lions were 6–4. Against the Los Angeles Rams, Detroit proved it was more than just a one-man team. Sanders only got 57 yards on 26 carries, but reserve quarterback Erik Kramer threw for 185 yards and 3 touchdowns, and the Lions won, 21–10. "We thought if we stopped Barry Sanders we would win the game," said Rams defensive back Todd Lyght. "But they made some big plays."

After beating Chicago and the New York Jets, Detroit was 10–4 and very close to making it into the postseason. By then Sanders had 16 touchdowns for the season, but he wanted to talk about how well the team was doing. He knew that very few people had expected the Lions to win ten games. "It's just an indication of how much better we are," he said.

Detroit needed a victory against the Green Bay Packers to make it into the playoffs. The Packers led, 10–7, at the half. Then, Kramer threw a pair of passes to Mike Farr that were good for 24 yards, down to the Green Bay 19-yard line. Kramer flipped a screen pass to Sanders, who was almost

Eyeing the opposing player, Barry Sanders lowers his shoulder and readies himself for the collision.

surrounded by five Packers. He faked, and ran his way for 17 yards to the 2-yard line. When he was stopped twice by the Green Bay line, Kramer lobbed the ball to Clark for the go-ahead touchdown. Mel Gray's 78-yard punt return for a touchdown later in the game ensured a 21–17 Lions win. Detroit was in the playoffs for the first time since 1983.

In the last regular game of the season, the Buffalo Bills thought they could beat Detroit by stacking the line to stop Sanders. But he still got 108 yards in 26 carries, and Detroit won, 17–14, on Eddie Murray's overtime field goal. The Bills' safety said it was easier to tackle water than to stop Sanders. "You can at least get in water's way. You know what direction it's going," he said. "I'm glad we only have to play him once." Sanders got one touchdown, to give him a total of 17 touchdowns for the season. That was a Lions record and the best in the league, but he lost the rushing title to Emmitt Smith of the

Dallas Cowboys. Smith gained 160 yards in his last game for 1,563 yards, fifteen yards better than Sanders.

The Cowboys were the Lions' first playoff opponents. Their game plan was to stack the line and bury Sanders every time he got the ball. If Sanders could be stopped, Dallas figured the Lions would be finished. Kramer said he looked at the game as a challenge. He was still filling in at quarterback for the injured Peete. Since the Cowboys would be looking for Sanders to get the ball on every play, the Lions would pass—and pass—and pass.

On the first drive, Kramer completed 4 of 5 passes for 68 yards and threw a touchdown. That was the way the whole game went. Kramer finished with 29 completed passes in 38 attempts for 341 yards and 3 touchdowns. Except for a 47-yard touchdown run late in the game, Sanders only gained 22 yards, but it did not matter because the Lions won, 38–6.

The Lions' season came to an abrupt halt the following week as they were whipped by Washington, 41–10. The Redskins forced a fumble and scored a touchdown within the first seventy-six seconds. After an interception, a field goal made the score 10–0 with just 4:02 gone. "The first quarter was something of a shock," said Detroit guard Ken Dallafior. "It was like walking into a snake pit."

The Redskins defense had a great game. "Barry was able to run outside on them a couple of times early in the game," said Kramer. "But they made an adjustment and wouldn't let him get outside after that."

It was a rough way to end a season, but the Lions were looking forward to more great years. "This has been a tremendous season," Fontes reminded reporters. "We have something to build on now. This club knows it has the stuff to be a winner for a long time."

As soon as the 1991 season was over, Sanders and his

With the snow falling, Sanders freezes the Pittsburgh Steelers defenders.

teammate Willie Green enrolled in a biology class at Oakland University, near Detroit. "I want to finish up what I started," Green said. "My old man used to say once you quit something, it becomes a habit." By then, Sanders was twenty-three years old. He had left Oklahoma State University after three years to sign with the Lions. He planned to take enough classes at Oakland to finish his degree and graduate from college.

Sanders did not make a big fuss about his college plans, just as he did not try to call attention to the hundreds of thousands of dollars he continued to give to the Paradise Baptist Church back in Wichita. "He gives without stipulation and without ulterior motives," said Reverend Paul L. Gray, Sr., the church's pastor. "Barry Sanders made it possible for a lower-income congregation to fulfill some dreams and expand our ministry. Where before we could dedicate $100 to shelter and feed the homeless, now we can give $1,000. We were able to increase our donations everywhere like that."

Sanders' sister Donna said people should not be surprised by his generosity. "Barry wasn't going to stop being a Christian just because he became a professional football player," she said. "And he didn't forget his home. He's got a great attachment here."

Paradise Church was building a new hall, which would be named for him. Wichita's youth football field had also been named for Sanders. Frank Smith, Wichita's director of parks and recreation, said that Sanders was an example for all the young people of his city.

Wichita councilman Rip Gooch said Sanders was more than just a great athlete. "We're all very proud of Barry here," he said. "He's not just a star football player. He's a role model for kids who are surrounded too much by drugs and gangs."

Chapter 6

Barry Sanders was healthy for the entire 1992 season, and he gained 1,352 yards. But after the playoff run in 1991, the season was a disappointment for the Detroit Lions. Their 5–11 record tied them for last in the Central Division of the National Football Conference.

The Lions hoped to get back in playoff contention in 1993. In the season opener against Atlanta, Rodney Peete completed 11 passes, new linebacker Pat Swilling harassed the Falcons offense all afternoon, and of course, Sanders sparked the offense.

Early in the game with the ball on the Atlanta 26-yard line, Sanders faked right, and the Falcons defense fell for it. Instantly, he switched direction and charged left. Nobody touched him.

Detroit finished the game with a 30–13 victory. After nine more games, his league-leading total of 1,052 yards was helping to keep the Lions in the race for a playoff spot. Unfortunately, Sanders sprained his left knee in a Thanksgiving Day game with the Chicago Bears. While he was sitting out the last five games of the regular season, his teammates fought their way into the playoffs, with a 10–6 mark.

Sanders was healed and ready for the playoff game with Green Bay. He cut and ran all over the Silverdome field, picking up 169 yards on 27 carries. Unfortunately, the Packers ruined his comeback by scoring a late come-from-behind touchdown to beat Detroit, 28–24.

The Lions were muddling through another mediocre season in 1994 when Sanders had an astonishing run against Tampa Bay. When he took the ball, he was grabbed by a Buccaneers lineman. The defender had a tight grip on Sanders' foot, but the Lions' star managed to break free. The would-be tackler was left on the turf empty-handed—except for Sanders' shoe. Sanders took off on one stockinged foot for 85 yards before he was finally brought down.

A few weeks later he had another great performance against Tampa Bay. By then, the Lions' new quarterback, Scott Mitchell, was out of action with a broken right hand. After a sloppy first half, the Bucs led, 3–0. That's when Sanders took control. He broke away for a 23-yard run that set up a one-run scoring plunge by Derrick Moore.

He was on his way to a long TD run of his own until Martin Mayhew grabbed his face mask and threw him to the turf. The 69-yard jaunt with the added penalty brought the ball to the Bucs' 9-yard line. On the next play, Dave Krieg, Mitchell's replacement, hit Brett Perriman for the score.

Sanders picked up 237 yards in that game, the best ever for a Lion. With ten games gone, he had 1,319 for the season. Fans and reporters began wondering if he was going to hit 2,000. Sanders said the big total was no big deal. "I have enough things to keep me occupied and busy without having to worry about the 2,000 yards." His number one goal, of course, was to get Detroit into the playoffs.

Sanders came up short in the last regular-season game when he only got 52 yards in a loss against the Miami Dolphins. That made his league-leading rushing total "only" 1,883, his best ever.

In the 1994 playoffs, the entire Packers team seemed to be waiting for him every time he got the ball. He carried it just 13 times for a total of minus one yard. It was his worst professional game. The Lions ended the season with a 16–13 loss.

In 1995, Detroit got revenge midway through the season by clipping Green Bay, 24–16. Mitchell hit Herman Moore for 3 touchdown passes, while Sanders picked up 167 yards in 22 carries.

Then, the team fell to a 3–6 record. William Clay Ford,

Sanders makes it a point to stay in shape. Staying physically fit has kept him injury free for most of his career.

Detroit's impatient owner, told Coach Wayne Fontes the Lions were good enough to make the playoffs again. If they did not, the coach would lose his job.

The Lions rallied, winning their last seven regular-season games. Sanders rushed for 1,500 yards. In the first playoff game, they faced their old quarterback, Peete, who had signed with the Philadelphia Eagles. It was a disaster. While Peete was throwing for 3 touchdowns, Mitchell was intercepted 4 times. The Lions were demolished, 58–37. "When you get your butt kicked," said Detroit linebacker Chris Spielman, "you get your butt kicked."

The Lions had high hopes for the 1996 season, but the team collapsed to a 5–11 record, despite Sanders' league-leading 1,553 yards. Fontes was fired and replaced by Bobby Ross.

But when the Lions began practicing for the 1997 season, Sanders was nowhere to be found. He refused to report to camp because he was upset about his contract. He was in the last year of a four-year, $17.2 million pact that paid him an average of $4.23 million a season. Sanders had thought that was plenty of money until quarterback Mitchell signed a four-year deal in February 1997 that guaranteed him $5.25 million a year.

Was Mitchell worth a million dollars more a year than Sanders? Hardly anybody thought so. After eight seasons of loyally doing his best for the team and piling up statistics matched by no other runner, Sanders thought he deserved to be the highest-paid player on the team. He refused to report until he got a new contract that met his terms.

Ross was mad. "Barry should be here," he said. "He's under contract." The coach was anxious to rebuild the team for a run at the playoffs. Sanders stuck to his guns. "I do feel bad about the strain it's maybe putting on Coach. I really like him.

I think he's going to be great for our team. But there's this other issue that has to be settled first."

Finally, on July 20, a week before exhibition games were scheduled to begin, Sanders and the Lions agreed to a five-year, $34.5 million contract. Sanders' new average yearly salary: $6.9 million. That made him the highest-paid player in the history of the NFL. Within a few days, quarterbacks such as Steve Young signed bigger contracts, but that did not change the fact that in Detroit, Barry Sanders was No. 1.

During the 1997 season, Sanders proved to be worth every penny. Sanders led the entire NFL in rushing, gaining a remarkable 2,053 yards. He was only the third player to ever rush for more than 2,000 yards in a season, joining Eric Dickerson and O. J. Simpson. That total also moved him up to second on the career-rushing list, trailing only the legendary Walter Payton.

The Lions also benefited from Sanders' great season. The team finished 9–7, and made the playoffs as a wild-card team. The Lions' opponent in the first round was the Tampa Bay Buccaneers. The Lions were able to keep the game close, but eventually fell to the Bucs, 20–10. After the season, it was announced that Sanders was the NFL's Co-MVP, along with Green Bay quarterback Brett Favre. Sanders was also named the NFL Player of the Year by *The Sporting News*.

Sanders had another strong year in 1998, rushing for almost 1,500 yards. The Lions, however, were dismal. Detroit finished the season 5-11, and it looked as if they were not making progress.

What came next was a shock to the football world. On July 28, 1999, Sanders announced his retirement just before the start of training camp. He said, "the reason I'm retiring is simple. My desire to leave the game is greater than my desire to remain in it." Sanders retired as one of the greatest players in

In 1997, Sanders became only the third player in NFL history to run for more than 2,000 yards in one season.

NFL history, and is a shoe-in for entry into the Pro Football Hall of Fame.

During his years in the NFL, Barry Sanders changed. When he came to Detroit, he was a twenty-year-old college kid from Wichita. Now he's a millionaire celebrity who's been one of the United States' most popular athletes for more than a decade.

Along with the fame and the money, Sanders has also had to deal with tragedy. In 1991, his older sister, Nancy, came to live with him. She was a talented, lively person who enjoyed singing and playing the piano. But she was dying from scleroderma, a painful skin disease. She died on November 6, 1991. "It's not how important life is," her little brother said. "But how important the experience of living life, with close ones and relatives, and how important that time is."

Sanders is still very close to the rest of his family. His parents still live in the huge home he bought for them in Kansas. He visits regularly. "I love it when he comes home," says his mother, Shirley. "We sit and talk for hours. I miss him. I feel for him sometimes—all the attention he gets and doesn't want."

Sanders' son, Barry James, was born April 10, 1994. B. J. lives with his mother in Oklahoma City. "I talk to him once or twice a week on the phone," Sanders said. "He tells me that some kid is pulling on his shirt in school. He's learning his ABC's and 1, 2, 3's. . . . He likes to talk . . . and he really likes daddy. That's cool. I like that."

The biggest change in Sanders since he became a professional athlete is his growing self-confidence and ability to be more outgoing. He seems to be enjoying himself more. He loves going to comedy clubs or to theaters to see plays. During the off-seasons he enjoyed traveling to Europe and Africa.

His former teammates joke that, even though he does not

Barry Sanders is a great player on the field and has always been a great role model.

like to spend money, he's starting to buy better clothes. "I was shocked," said Perriman. "The main thing is, he's wearing clothes that match."

Despite the changes, Barry Sanders is still a far cry from being a spoiled superstar. It's not unusual for him to play basketball with strangers at a gym without their discovering who he is. When he ate dinner at the home of his former teammate Lomas Brown, "most of the time Barry would be with my kids sitting on the floor playing a video game or eating off their plates watching a movie," Brown said.

Of course, William Sanders is still very proud of his son—the way he played and the way he behaves. Mr. Sanders used to travel the country to watch the Lions. Once, when he was in Dallas, he was introduced to Emmitt Smith. The Cowboys superstar promised to autograph a football for Mr. Sanders after the game. But after the Lions took an overtime victory, Smith refused.

"My Barry would never do that," said the proud father.

Career Statistics

YEAR	TEAM	RUSHING				PASS RECEIVING			
		Carries	Yards	Avg.	TD	Rec.	Yards	Avg.	TD
1989	Detroit	280	1,470	5.3	14	24	282	11.8	0
1990	Detroit	255	*1,304*	5.1	13	36	480	13.3	3
1991	Detroit	342	1,548	4.5	*16*	41	307	7.5	1
1992	Detroit	312	1,352	4.3	9	29	225	7.8	1
1993	Detroit	243	1,115	4.6	3	36	205	5.7	0
1994	Detroit	331	*1,883*	5.7	7	44	283	6.4	1
1995	Detroit	314	1,500	4.8	11	48	398	8.3	1
1996	Detroit	307	*1,553*	5.1	11	24	147	6.1	0
1997	Detroit	335	*2,053*	6.1	11	33	305	9.2	3
1998	Detroit	343	1,491	4.3	4	37	289	7.8	0
Totals		3,062	15,269	5.0	99	352	2,921	8.3	10

Avg.=Average
TD=Touchdowns
Rec.=Receptions
Italics=League Leader

Where to Write Barry Sanders:

Mr. Barry Sanders
c/o NFL Players Association
2021 L Street, NW, Suite 600
Washington, DC 20036

On the Internet at:
http://www.nfl.com/Lions/news/sanders_retrospective_index.html
http://www.nfl.com/players/stats/career/2853.html

Index